OUTSTANDING AFRICAN AMERICANS

GREAT AFRICAN AMERICANS IN

HISTORY

CARLOTTA HACKER

Crabtree Publishing Company

Dedication

This series is dedicated to the African-American men and women who followed their dreams. With courage, faith, and hard work, they overcame obstacles in their lives and went on to excel in their fields. They set standards as some of the best Olympic athletes in the world. They brought innovation to film, jazz, and the arts, and the world is richer for their touch. They became leaders, and through their example encouraged hope and self-reliance. *Outstanding African Americans* is both an acknowledgment of and a tribute to these people.

Project Manager
Lauri Seidlitz

Production Manager
Amanda Howard

Editor
Virginia Mainprize

Copy Editor
Janice Parker

Design
Warren Clark

Layout
Chris Bowerman

Photograph Credits
Cover: Carver photo (Corbis-Bettmann), Coleman photo (Underwood/Bettmann), Henson photo (Corbis-Bettmann); **Bettmann Archive:** pages 8, 11, 22; **Charles L. Blockson Afro-American Collection, Temple University:** pages 9, 28, 46; **Corbis-Bettmann:** pages 34 (Robert Savon Pious), 7, 12, 27, 29, 37, 38, 45; **Dusable Museum of African American History, Chicago, Illinois:** pages 42, 44; **Globe Photos:** page 31; **National Air and Space Museum, Smithsonian Institution:** pages 17 (88-7993), 18 (84-14782), 21 (85-7754); **Schomburg Center for Research in Black Culture, New York Public Library:** pages 4, 5, 13, 15, 19, 20, 23, 24, 26, 30, 35, 39, 41, 52, 55, 58, 61; **Underwood & Underwood/Corbis-Bettmann:** page 16; **UPI/Corbis-Bettmann:** pages 33 (Ron Bennett), 6, 14, 25, 32, 36, 49; **U.S. Department of the Interior:** page 10; **Visual Image Presentations:** page 40.

Every reasonable effort has been made to trace ownership and to obtain permission to reprint copyright material. The publishers would be pleased to have any errors or omissions brought to their attention so that they may be corrected in subsequent printings.

Published by
Crabtree Publishing Company

350 Fifth Avenue,	360 York Road, R.R. 4	73 Lime Walk
Suite 3308	Niagara-on-the-Lake	Headington
New York, NY	Ontario, Canada	Oxford OX3 7AD
U.S.A. 10018	L0S 1J0	United Kingdom

Cataloging-in-Publication Data

Hacker, Carlotta.
    Great African Americans in history / Carlotta Hacker.
      p.   cm. — (Outstanding African Americans)
    Includes index.
    Summary: Profiles thirteen African Americans who have excelled in various fields, including medicine, science, civil rights, and exploration.
    ISBN 0-86505-805-9 (RLB). — ISBN 0-86505-819-9 (pbk.)
    1. Afro-Americans—Biography—Juvenile literature. 2. Afro-Americans—History—Juvenile literature. [1. Afro-Americans—Biography.] I. Title. II. Series.
    E185.96.H13   1997
    920'.009296073—dc20
    [B]
                                   96-38690
                                     CIP
                                     AC

Contents

For other great African Americans in history, see the book

GREAT AFRICAN AMERICANS IN CIVIL RIGHTS
Martin Luther King, Jr. • Thurgood Marshall • Rosa Parks • Malcolm X...and others!

Mary McLeod Bethune

Personality Profile

Career: Teacher and civil rights activist.

Born: July 10, 1875, in Mayesville, South Carolina, to Samuel and Patsy McLeod.

Died: May 18, 1955, in Daytona Beach, Florida.

Family: Married Albertus Bethune, 1897, (separated). Had one son, Albert.

Education: Trinity Presbyterian Mission School, 1886; Scotia Seminary, 1894; Moody Bible Institute, 1895.

Awards: Spingarn Medal, National Association for the Advancement of Colored People (NAACP), 1935; Frances Drexel Award for Distinguished Service, 1937; Thomas Jefferson Award, 1942; Medal of Honor and Merit (Haiti), 1949; Star of Africa (Liberia), 1952; honorary degrees from several universities.

Growing Up

When Mary was seven, she picked up a book in the house where her mother worked. The white owner's daughter snatched it from her. "You don't need that," she said, "Negroes can't read." From that moment on, Mary was determined to learn to read.

At first, this seemed an impossible dream. Mary's parents were former slaves who could spare no money for their children's education. They had a tiny farm in Mayesville, South Carolina. To earn a little extra money to help support the family, Mary and her brothers and sisters picked cotton for white plantation owners. Mary learned to pick cotton when she was four or five years old.

In 1885, when Mary was ten, she had a bit of luck. A church mission school for blacks had opened a few miles away. For two happy years, Mary studied there. She did so well that the principal arranged for her to attend Scotia Seminary, the mission's boarding school for African-American girls in North Carolina. Many of the students went on to be teachers, but Mary decided she wanted to be a missionary. She completed her education at the Moody Bible Institute in Chicago. She was the only black student.

"I rang doorbells…. If a prospect refused to make a contribution, I would say, 'Thank you for your time.' No matter how deep my hurt, I always smiled. I refused to be discouraged, for neither God nor man could use a discouraged soul."

Developing Skills

"Our aim must be to create a world of fellowship and justice where no man's skin color is held against him."

Mary hoped to be a missionary in Africa, but she was not accepted. Only white missionaries were sent to Africa, she was told. Mary was very disappointed. She wanted to do something really good with her life. Then she realized that she did not have to go to Africa. There was great need for her help at home.

After teaching for a few years in Georgia, Mary started a mission school in Palatka, Florida. Then she heard about the railway that was being built on Florida's east coast. Black laborers had crowded into the area, hoping to get work. Many had brought their families with them. They lived in terrible conditions. There was no proper housing and no schools for the children.

Mary decided to start a school in Daytona Beach. She rented an old frame house, scrubbed it spotless, and then opened for business. She called her school the Daytona Normal and Industrial School for Negro Girls. When it opened in 1904, it had only five students. Two years later, there were 250 students. In 1923, it joined with a boy's school to become Bethune-Cookman College.

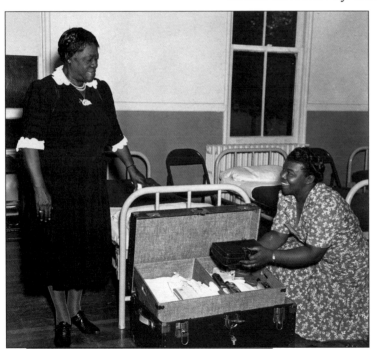

As the Assistant Director of the Women's Army Auxiliary Corps (WAAC), Mary greets a new member.

During her first years in Daytona Beach, Mary did far more than teach school. She organized a hospital for African Americans, started a training school for black nurses, and opened a playground for local children. If Mary saw anything that needed doing, she did it.

Soon, Mary's activities spread far beyond Daytona Beach. In 1935, she formed the National Council of Negro Women. By then, she was respected throughout the nation as an expert on education. Under Presidents Coolidge and Hoover, Mary went to Washington as national advisor on child welfare. President Franklin Roosevelt made her Director of the Division of Minority Affairs, an organization set up to help young people.

Mary addresses the crowds in Madison Square Garden, New York City.

Accomplishments

1904 Founded Daytona Normal and Industrial School.

1920 Vice-president of the National Urban League.

1923 Merged her school with a boy's school to form Bethune-Cookman College.

1924-28 President of National Association of Colored Women.

1935 Formed National Council of Negro Women and became its president.

1936-43 Director of Division of Minority Affairs, National Youth Administration.

1945 Special representative for U.S. State Department at the conference that formed the United Nations.

1952 Traveled to Africa to represent the United States at the inauguration of William Tubman as president of Liberia.

1974 A seventeen-foot statue was erected in Washington, D.C., in her memory and honor.

Overcoming Obstacles

When Mary started her school in Daytona Beach, she had no money to run it. By cooking pies and selling them to railway workers, she had earned just enough to rent the building. At first, she used wooden boxes as desks. She made ink from wild berry juice. She made pencils out of charred firewood. She furnished the school by picking through the town's garbage dumps.

Next, Mary went from door to door asking for money. It took a lot of work and courage, but it brought in the needed funds. Many people, white as well as black, took an interest in the school and were glad to help support it.

To feed her students, Mary started a farm. Teachers and students worked together to grow the food they needed. The students also earned money for the school by singing in hotels and clubs. They even sang in the local jails.

As the school grew, more buildings were needed and a larger campus had to be bought. In her search for funds, Mary gained the support of two white millionaires. With their help, the school was able to stay open, even during the hard years of the Great Depression.

Artist Betsy Graves Reyneau's painting of Mary, 1944.

When Mary started the school in 1904, she taught only the basics: reading, writing, religion, and some useful skills, such as sewing. By the 1930s, the students were learning a wide range of subjects. In 1934, sixty-four students completed their junior college courses. By 1942, the school had become a senior college. Today, it has more than two thousand students.

Mary believed every child should have a good education.

Mary kept up her interest in the college even when she was busy with national affairs in Washington. When she died in 1955, just two months before her eightieth birthday, she was buried on the college grounds. Many people consider her one of the most powerful black women in American history.

Special Interests

- Mary had a flare for fashion. She often dressed in long capes and velvets, and carried a cane.
- In her later years, Mary enjoyed traveling and fulfilled a lifelong dream by visiting Africa in 1952.

George Washington Carver

Personality Profile

Career: Agricultural scientist.

Born: 1864, near Diamond, Missouri, to Mary and a fellow slave.

Died: January 5, 1943, in Tuskegee, Alabama.

Education: Simpson College, Iowa; B.S., Iowa Agricultural College, 1894; M.S., Iowa State College, 1896.

Awards: Elected a Fellow of the Royal Society of Arts, Great Britain, 1916; Spingarn Medal, National Association for the Advancement of Colored People (NAACP), 1922; Theodore Roosevelt Medal, 1939; George Washington Carver Monument erected at his birthplace, 1951.

Growing Up

In the last months of the Civil War, when he was less than a year old, George and his mother were kidnapped from the Missouri homestead where she was a slave. In those days, slaves were sometimes stolen and sold to other plantation owners. George's mother was never seen again. Her white owners rescued George and raised him and his brother Jim as their own children.

George's foster parents were Moses and Susan Carver. Although they had little money, they did their best for the boys. Since George longed to learn to read, they sent him to the nearest school for black children that was more than ten miles away. The local school did not allow African Americans to attend. George started there in 1874, when he was ten, but he was twenty years old before he graduated from high school. He had to keep leaving school to earn money to support himself.

Throughout his teenage years, George traveled from place to place, taking whatever work he could get. His jobs ranged from gardening and fruit picking to cooking and doing laundry. If there was no work in one town, George moved on to another. Sometimes he had no place to sleep. Often he went hungry. He saved up his money until he could go back to school for another term.

"It has always been the one great ideal of my life to be of the greatest good to the greatest number of my people."

Developing Skills

A fter graduating from high school, George was determined to go to college, though he knew it would not be easy. Although slavery had been abolished, most universities accepted only white students. For a time, George worked as a farmer. In his spare time, he sketched plants as a hobby. Eventually, he was accepted by Simpson College in Indianola, Iowa.

George studied painting at Simpson. It was his favorite subject, and he was good at it. But the painting teacher soon persuaded him to learn something more practical. She knew he would have difficulty finding work as an artist.

With her help, he enrolled at Iowa Agricultural College at Ames, Iowa. After getting his Bachelor's degree, he was made assistant botanist at the college's research station. After his Master's degree, he was appointed to teach agriculture at Tuskegee Institute in Alabama.

George experimenting in the lab.

Tuskegee Institute had been started in the 1880s as an industrial and agricultural school for African Americans. When George arrived there in 1896, it was only a collection of shacks. George was shocked at the state of the place. There was no proper laboratory. He had to make his own equipment out of old bottles and bits of wire.

As well as teaching, George traveled through the South, helping farmers grow better crops. Many farmers were struggling because cotton was no longer selling well. George suggested that they grow peanuts, soybeans, and sweet potatoes.

To help farmers sell what they grew, George researched new ways of using their crops. George's peanut research was especially famous. He discovered more than 300 products that could be made from peanuts. These included soap, face powder, and metal polish, as well as more than a hundred recipes.

When George started his research, peanuts were not a major crop. By the time of his death, they had become a $200-million-a-year industry.

Born of slave parents, George went on to become a famous scientist.

Accomplishments

1886-88 Homesteaded in Kansas.

1891-96 Studied for B.S. and M.S. degrees at Iowa Agricultural College.

1896 Appointed to Tuskegee Institute to teach agriculture.

1897 Started an agricultural experimental station at Tuskegee.

1899 Began visiting farmers to give advice on growing crops.

1903-10 Published many bulletins on growing and cooking sweet potatoes and other crops.

1906 Established a well-equipped traveling school to give instruction to farmers.

1916 Published *How to Grow the Peanut and 105 Ways of Preparing It for Human Consumption.*

1921 Spoke to a congressional committee about the benefits of peanut growing.

Overcoming Obstacles

George faced many problems throughout his life. Lack of money was one. While he was a student, he had to earn money to support himself. He took in laundry—scrubbing shirts far into the night. Later, as a teacher at Tuskegee, he was constantly in need of funds for his agricultural experiments. As a result, much of his research focused on finding inexpensive ways of farming.

Racism was strong and widespread at that time. George came up against it when he first applied to college. After being accepted by Highland College in northeastern Kansas, he saved every penny to get there. But when the people at the college saw him and realized he was African American, they refused him admission.

Automobile millionaire Henry Ford presented George with a fully-equipped laboratory for food research in 1942.

Even when he was finally accepted by a college, George still faced racism. As the first black student at the Iowa Agricultural Institute, he was not at first given a room nor allowed to eat with the other students. As the months passed, the students began to see George as a friend, not just an African American. His quiet dignity impressed them, and soon he was accepted as an equal.

Even at the end of his life, when he was a famous scientist, George suffered racial insults. In 1930, for example, he was asked to leave the lobby of the New Yorker Hotel. He was told there were no vacant rooms. He refused to leave. Dignified and determined, he stayed there until the manager arrived. The manager recognized him and said there was indeed room for him in the hotel.

By the 1930s, George was not only famous, he was also quite wealthy. Shortly before he died, he donated all his savings to set up the George Washington Carver Foundation for agricultural research at Tuskegee Institute.

George discovered over 300 products that could be made from peanuts.

Special Interests

- George loved to paint and was very good at it. His drawing of a yucca plant received an honorable mention at the Chicago World's Fair in 1893.

Bessie Coleman

Personality Profile

Career: Aviator.

Born: January 26, 1892, in Atlanta, Texas, to Susan and George Coleman. Some sources state Bessie was born in 1893 or 1896.

Died: April 30, 1926, in Jacksonville, Florida.

Education: Langston Industrial College; Burnham's School of Beauty Culture.

Honors: She is honored each year on Memorial Day by African-American pilots who fly in formation over Lincoln Cemetery and drop flowers on her grave; many Bessie Coleman Aero Clubs were formed after her death, and an organization called the Bessie Coleman Aviators was formed by black women pilots in the Chicago area, 1975.

Growing Up

When Bessie was born, no one in the world had ever flown an airplane. Bessie certainly never dreamed that she would do so. She grew up in Waxahachie, Texas, "the cotton capital of the West." Like her mother and brothers and sisters, Bessie spent much of her childhood working in the cotton fields. All the Coleman children had to work because their father had left home when Bessie was seven.

During slow periods, when there was little work in the cotton fields, the Coleman children went to school. Bessie's mother was determined that they would have an education. Bessie was good at math, so she was given the job of bookkeeping for the cotton plantation. She also took in laundry, to earn enough money to go to college.

After leaving high school, Bessie enrolled at Langston Industrial College, a school for African Americans. She hoped to train as a teacher but had to leave after a year because she ran out of money. She moved to Chicago where two of her brothers were living. There she took a course in manicuring—learning how to shape and polish people's fingernails. Her first real job was as a manicurist at the White Sox Barber Shop in Chicago.

"I knew we [African Americans] had no aviators, neither men nor women, and I knew the Race needed to be represented along this most important line, so I thought it my duty to risk my life to learn aviation and to encourage flying among men and women of our Race."

Developing Skills

After working for a while at the White Sox Barber Shop, Bessie became manager of a chili restaurant. This was around 1919, just after the end of World War I. In both the barber shop and the restaurant, the customers talked excitedly about the new flying machines that had been invented by the brothers Wilbur and Orville Wright in 1903. Since then, there had been many advances, and airplanes had played an important role in the war.

Bessie was the first black woman to become a licenced airplane pilot.

Bessie longed to fly in an airplane. In fact, she longed to pilot one. No African-American woman had ever piloted an aircraft. Nor were there more than a few women pilots in the entire world. Neither of these facts stopped Bessie. She was determined to learn to fly.

Bessie had a hard time getting started. No American flying school would admit her. They were only for whites. Yet Bessie persisted, and eventually the editor of the *Chicago Defender* heard about her. He paid for Bessie to go to a flying school in France. There she not only learned to fly but also to jump by parachute and to do stunts with an airplane. In 1922, she became the first black woman to receive her international pilot's licence. It allowed her to fly anywhere in the world, including the United States.

In the 1920s, it was almost impossible for any woman, black or white, to get a job as a pilot in a passenger airplane. So Bessie made her living by barnstorming—doing stunts to thrill the crowds at fairs and exhibitions. Her first appearance was at an air show at Curtiss Field, near New York City, in 1922. The crowds loved it. She became known as Brave Bessie. People flocked to see this brilliant young aviator.

Brave Bessie's stunts drew many crowds to her air shows.

Bessie's flying career was indeed brilliant, but it was all too brief. In 1926, while her mechanic was piloting the plane, it suddenly spun out of control. Bessie was not wearing a seat belt, and she was thrown from the plane at 2,000 feet. She was just over thirty when she died. However, she had already become a role model for generations of young African-American women.

Accomplishments

1915 Trained as a manicurist in Chicago.	**1922-26** Performed at many air shows and carnivals.
1920 Went to France to train as a pilot.	**1926** Forced the Orlando Chamber of Commerce to admit African Americans to their air show.
1921 Awarded pilot's licence in France.	
1922 Awarded international pilot's licence.	

Overcoming Obstacles

Even after Bessie got her pilot's licence, she continued to face racial discrimination. This was especially so in the South, even though she had become a famous barnstormer. Although she was booked to fly for the Negro Welfare League's show in Florida, she could not get a plane. No Florida dealer would rent or lend a plane to an African American. Bessie had to call her white mechanic in Texas to help her. He rented a plane there and flew it to Florida.

On another occasion, when Bessie was booked to fly for the Orlando Chamber of Commerce, she discovered that African Americans would not be allowed to watch. The air show was for whites only. Bessie said that she would not fly in the show. The Chamber of Commerce gave in and agreed to allow African Americans onto the field. At Bessie's request, pilots were sent up to drop information sheets letting African Americans know they could come to watch the show.

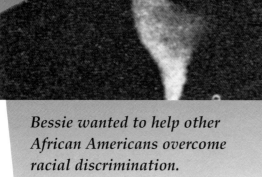

Bessie wanted to help other African Americans overcome racial discrimination.

By taking a stand against racism, Bessie risked losing work. She needed the money because she was hoping to start a flying school for African Americans.

Although Bessie did not live long enough to start her training school, she did achieve her aim of encouraging other African Americans to fly. Through her example, many other people decided that they would become pilots. Within a few years of Bessie's death, there were black fliers throughout America. They formed Bessie Coleman Aero Clubs, and in 1930, the clubs started a monthly magazine, the *Bessie Coleman Aero News*. In 1990, a monument was unveiled at Lambert-St. Louis International Airport. It celebrates seventy-five African Americans, including Bessie, who have made a special contribution to aviation.

Bessie's example inspired many women to learn to fly.

Special Interests

- Bessie studied French before traveling to France to learn how to fly.
- Bessie's nickname was Queen Bess, Daredevil Aviatrix.

W.E.B. Du Bois

Family: Married Nina Gomer, 1896, (died, 1950); married Shirley Graham, 1951. By his first marriage, he had a son, Burghardt, and a daughter, Nina; by his second marriage, he had a stepson, David.

Education: Great Barrington High School, 1884; B.A., Fisk University, 1888; M.A., Harvard University, 1891; Ph.D., Harvard University, 1895.

Awards: Spingarn Medal, National Association for the Advancement of Colored People (NAACP), 1932; elected to the National Institute of Arts and Letters, 1943; awarded Lenin International Peace Prize, 1958; received honorary degrees from Fisk and other universities; honored by African countries, including Liberia, which made him a Knight Commander of the Liberian Human Order of African Redemption.

Personality Profile

Career: Social activist, author, editor, and teacher.

Born: February 23, 1868, in Great Barrington, Massachusetts, to Alfred and Mary Du Bois.

Died: August 27, 1963, in Accra, Ghana.

Growing Up

William was descended from French, Dutch, and African ancestors. He longed to be a writer from his earliest years. By the time he was fifteen, he was writing for two African-American newspapers. In high school, he was an excellent scholar and was respected by his fellow students, both black and white.

William first became concerned about racial problems after he won a scholarship to Fisk University in 1885. At Fisk, all the students were black, and courses in black studies were offered. William was angered by what he learned about the sufferings of African Americans. He was also shocked by the terrible state of the local black schools. He saw these schools firsthand because he taught in them during his summer vacations.

After graduating from Fisk, William went to Harvard University. He paid for his courses with scholarships and grants. He hoped to complete his education with two years in Europe, but the university would not give a grant for a black student to study abroad. William wrote an angry letter to the president of the university. To his surprise, the president gave in, and William was awarded a grant of $750. He spent two years at the University of Berlin. After his return in 1894, he completed his thesis and became the first African American to get a Ph.D. from Harvard.

"Am I an American or am I a Negro? Can I be both?"

Developing Skills

On his twenty-fifth birthday, William wrote in his diary that he hoped to make a name for himself in science and literature "and thus raise my race." He spent much of his life as a professor, teaching at a number of universities. He also edited magazines and newspapers and wrote many scholarly papers and books. One of these books was *The Souls of Black Folk*, a collection of essays about the unequal treatment of African Americans.

Most of William's writings were about racism. They brought him a lot of attention, but they did not much improve the situation of African Americans. He realized he would have to find another way to protest if he were to have a real effect. With other black leaders, he formed the Niagara Movement in 1905. Its aim was to end racism and give all African Americans the same rights as whites.

This aim was very different from that of another black leader, Booker T. Washington. Booker believed that equality could wait. His first goal was to train African Americans in skills so that they could earn a living. Some black reformers agreed with Booker. Others agreed with William. To try to heal this split, William helped found the National Association for the Advancement of Colored People (NAACP) in 1910. The NAACP included whites as well as blacks and had many powerful supporters.

William worked as a professor at a number of universities.

As William grew older, he became concerned about Africa as well as America. Much of Africa was still controlled by Britain, France, and other European countries. William said these countries should give Africa back to the Africans. To help this come about, he attended many overseas meetings.

In the mid-1960s, many African colonies became independent countries. William saw only the beginning of this process when he died in 1963.

William at the World Peace Conference in Paris, France.

Accomplishments

1897-1910 Professor of history and economics, University of Atlanta.

1903 Published *The Souls of Black Folk*.

1905 Founded the Niagara Movement.

1910 Helped found the NAACP.

1910-1934 Director of publicity for the NAACP and editor of *Crisis*, the NAACP paper.

1934-44 Head of department of sociology, University of Atlanta.

1944-48 Director of research for the NAACP.

1945 NAACP delegate to conference that founded the United Nations.

1948-51 Co-chairperson of Council on African Affairs.

1950 Director of Peace Information Center, New York City.

Overcoming Obstacles

B ecause William spoke out so boldly, he made enemies as well as friends. He quarreled with Booker T. Washington about what was best for black Americans. Later, he quarreled with fellow members of the NAACP. This was because he decided that African Americans would be better off with segregation rather than integration. In other words, he thought that if white people would not give African Americans equal treatment, African Americans should get together and help themselves. Blacks should establish separate schools, churches, hospitals, army training camps, and so on. He believed this type of segregation would give African Americans more power.

William was one of the founders of the National Association for the Advancement of Colored People (NAACP).

When William expressed these views in the NAACP paper *Crisis*, there was a great outcry. He had to resign as editor of the paper. He also resigned from the board of the NAACP. Later, he rejoined the NAACP, and in the 1940s, he represented it at the conference that formed the United Nations.

As William grew older, he began to think communism would solve America's problems. He visited communist China and the Soviet Union, and he liked what he saw there. Low-income Chinese and Russians seemed to have a better life than low-income Americans. Because William spoke in favor of communism, he was accused of being a spy. Some people called him a traitor.

The American government took away William's passport to stop him from traveling. None of this silenced William. He continued to organize meetings and write papers. In 1961, he joined the Communist Party.

William's passport was eventually returned to him, and he was free to travel again. He chose to spend his last years in Africa. William moved to the country of Ghana in 1961 at the invitation of the president. When he died two years later, at the age of ninety-five, he was given a state funeral.

Right until the end of his life, William continued to call for better conditions for his people. He inspired Martin Luther King, Jr., and other leaders of the civil rights movement. These younger men and women later achieved many of the reforms that William had worked for all his life.

William with his wife, Shirley Graham.

Special Interests

- William traveled to the Soviet Union and China in the 1950s where he learned about the communist system of government.

Matthew Henson

Personality Profile

Career: Explorer.

Born: August 6, 1866, in Charles County, Maryland, to Lemuel and Caroline Henson.

Died: March 9, 1955, in New York City, New York.

Family: Married Lucy Ross, 1907. Had one son, Anaukaq, by his Inuit friend, Ahkahtingwaq.

Awards: Congressional Medal, 1944; Gold Medal of the Geographical Society of Chicago, 1948; Presidential Citation, 1954; several other medals and honorary degrees from schools, including Morgan State College and Howard University.

Growing Up

Matthew hardly knew his parents. Both of them died before he was eight. He was raised by an uncle in Washington, D.C., who sent him to school occasionally. Most of the time, he washed dishes in a restaurant. Sometimes he served the customers. His favorite customer was a sailor named Baltimore Jack. Matthew loved to listen to the tales Baltimore Jack told about life at sea.

In 1879, when Matthew was thirteen, he decided that he would go to sea. He walked to Baltimore, Maryland, and convinced the captain of a ship, the *Katie Hines*, to hire him as a cabin boy. The captain became very fond of Matthew and treated him like a son. He taught him to read and write and trained him to become a sailor. For six years, Matthew sailed the seas, visiting China, Africa, and other far-off places. When the captain died, Matthew returned to the United States.

Matthew had gained many skills during his years at sea, so he had no difficulty finding work. But the work seemed dull compared to his life as a sailor. He longed for something more exciting. He was determined that somehow he would get away again and have more adventures.

> *"As in the past, from the beginning of history, wherever the world's work was done by a white man, he had been accompanied by a colored man."*

Developing Skills

"The Commander gave the word, 'We will plant the stars and stripes—at the North Pole!' and it was done."

Matthew's big chance came when he was working in a hat shop in Washington, D.C. One day, the explorer Robert Peary came into the store to buy a helmet for an expedition to Nicaragua. As Robert talked, he mentioned that he was looking for a personal servant to go with him. By the time he left the hat shop, he had found one—Matthew.

Matthew spent the next twenty-two years exploring with Robert. From the very first, he was far more than a servant. He was quick to learn new skills. He already spoke several languages and easily learned new ones. He was just the person for an expedition, whether it was in the jungle or the Arctic.

After Nicaragua, all their expeditions were in the Arctic. In 1898, they set out to find the North Pole. Nobody had yet traveled as far north as the North Pole, although many people had tried. Robert and Matthew went three times. On their second attempt, in 1905-06, they came within 175 miles of the Pole.

On their third trip, in 1908-09, Robert and Matthew at last succeeded. On April 6, 1909, Matthew was out in front. When Robert caught up with him, Matthew announced, "I think I am the first person to sit on the top of the world." Robert was annoyed and said the North Pole was three miles farther. He continued to search for the North Pole himself, accompanied by two Inuit.

Matthew had traveled to many places around the world before he helped discover the North Pole.

When Robert returned to camp and Matthew tried to congratulate him, Robert would not shake hands. From then on, Robert was no longer friendly with Matthew. When the expedition came home to America, Robert took all the credit for himself, claiming that he alone discovered the North Pole. He made no mention of Matthew. Robert was treated as a hero. Matthew was ignored.

Matthew is seen here holding the American flag as the expedition recorded its accomplishment.

Many years passed before Matthew's role was recognized. Honors came only towards the end of his life. After his death, he received further honors. The first of these was in 1961 when the state of Maryland placed a bronze plaque in his name in the State House, Annapolis. The plaque proclaimed that Matthew Henson was the co-discoverer of the North Pole.

Accomplishments

1887 Expedition to Nicaragua.

1891-1909 Seven expeditions to the Arctic.

1909 Co-discoverer of the North Pole.

1912 Published *A Negro Explorer at the North Pole*.

1913-36 Employed as a clerk at U.S. Customs House, New York City.

1944 Awarded a Congressional Medal for his participation in the 1908-09 expedition to the Pole.

1947 Published *Dark Companion*.

1961 Honored as co-discoverer of the North Pole by the state of Maryland.

1988 Hero's burial in Arlington Cemetery.

Overcoming Obstacles

O n their way home from the North Pole in 1909, Robert told Matthew he was not to give lectures about their adventures. Robert wanted all the credit, and he did not want Matthew to tell his own story of the events. Matthew kept silent for twelve years. When at last he began to give lectures, it was only because he badly needed the money.

Matthew was featured in the first issue of **Negro Heroes,** *the first African-American magazine in comic picture form.*

Until then, Matthew carried on as well as he could. At first, he worked as a parking-lot attendant. He did not complain, but some of his friends did. They told President Taft about him, and the president found Matthew a job in a U.S. Customs House in New York City.

In 1912, Matthew wrote the book *A Negro Explorer at the North Pole.* Even this did not bring him fame. People expected explorers to be white. On the few occasions when Matthew was mentioned in accounts of the expedition, he was referred to as Robert's "Negro servant." This was very unfair because Matthew was a highly experienced explorer. Before setting out on the last expedition, Robert had said of Matthew, "He must go with me. I cannot make it without him."

Gradually, Matthew did become known as an explorer. In 1937, he was elected to the Explorers Club, and in 1944, he was given a Congressional Medal in honor of his journey to the North Pole. In 1947, with the help of Bradley Robinson, Matthew wrote *Dark Companion*. This book was more successful than his first, and it brought him further attention. In 1950 and 1954, he was honored at White House ceremonies.

Matthew was given a hero's burial in Arlington Cemetery in 1988, thirty-three years after his death.

When Matthew died in 1955, his family tried to get him buried in Arlington National Cemetery. They were told it was impossible because Matthew had never been in the armed services. His body lay in an ordinary cemetery until April 6, 1988. Exactly seventy-nine years after he helped discover the North Pole, his body was given a hero's burial at Arlington.

Special Interests

- In Matthew's years on the ship *Katie Hines*, he traveled to China, North Africa, and Europe.
- Matthew learned to speak many languages during his travels.

Harriet Tubman

Personality Profile

Career: Underground Railroad leader and social reformer.

Born: Around 1820, in Dorchester County, Maryland, to Benjamin and Harriet Ross.

Died: March 10, 1913, In Auburn, New York.

Family: John Tubman, 1844, (died, 1867); married Nelson Davis, 1869, (died, 1889).

Honors: A liberty ship was named Harriet Tubman during World War II; the U.S. Postal Service issued a Harriet Tubman stamp, 1978; there have been many other honors and memorials.

Because she had served in the Civil War, Harriet applied for a government pension. This proved to be the longest of all her struggles. It took her thirty years before the government finally granted her a pension of twenty dollars a month.

Harriet used the money to buy land in Auburn, New York. She opened a home for elderly ex-slaves who were too old to support themselves. With the help of local church groups, she established the Harriet Tubman Home for Aged and Indigent Colored People. It was dedicated as a national historic landmark in 1975.

Harriet opened a home in New York state for elderly ex-slaves.

Special Interests

- Harriet supported the women's rights movement in the 1890s. She was a strong supporter of Susan B. Anthony, a leader in the campaign to get women the right to vote.
- Harriet had a strong belief in God that she felt gave her the courage to work on the Underground Railroad.

Daniel Hale Williams

Personality Profile

Career: Surgeon.

Born: January 18, 1856, in Hollidaysburg, Pennsylvania, to Daniel and Sarah Williams.

Died: August 4, 1931, in Idlewild, Michigan.

Family: Married Alice Johnson, 1898, (died, 1924).

Education: Haire's Classical Academy, 1878; Chicago Medical College, 1883.

Growing Up

Daniel's ancestors had African-American, Native American, and European backgrounds. One of his grandmothers was a Scottish-Irish woman. His other grandmother had been a slave on the same plantation as the famous reformer Frederick Douglass. Daniel's father and grandfather were barbers in Hollidaysburg, Pennsylvania.

In 1866, when Daniel was ten, his father died, leaving the family very short of money. Since Daniel was too young to train as a barber, he was sent to Baltimore to live with a family friend and learn shoemaking. He hated it and ran away. He took the train to Rockford, Illinois, where his mother and sisters had gone.

In Rockford, Daniel learned the barber's trade while also attending school. He found barbering almost as unpleasant as shoemaking. What he really wanted to be was a doctor.

One of the most famous doctors in the area was Henry Palmer, who had run the largest military hospital during the Civil War. At the age of twenty-two, Daniel became one of Dr. Palmer's apprentices. It was on-the-job training. The apprentices learned medicine and surgery by helping the doctor with his work. Daniel received such good training that he was accepted by the Chicago Medical School in 1880. He graduated three years later.

"We have the material, the brains, and the ambition in our men and women to accomplish the highest results in any line of work."

Developing Skills

After graduating, Daniel opened a medical office in Chicago. He had read of the discoveries of Louis Pasteur in France and Joseph Lister in England, and he put their ideas into action. This involved using antiseptics to kill germs. At the time, most surgeons made no attempt to sterilize their instruments to make them free of germs. Some even kept their knives and scalpels in their jacket pockets. As a result, wounds often became infected after an operation, and many patients died.

Daniel kept his office spotlessly clean. He sprayed the room with carbolic acid, a strong germ killer. To sterilize his instruments, he boiled them in water. Before long, several Chicago clinics hired him as a visiting doctor. In 1889, he was appointed to the Illinois Board of Health.

One of Daniel's goals was to open a hospital in Chicago that would accept all races, both as patients and as doctors and nurses. In those days blacks could not be patients in hospitals, except in the charity wards. Also, most African Americans did not have the chance to get first-rate medical training and could not work in hospitals.

The original Provident Hospital, shown here in 1898, where black men and women could be trained as doctors and nurses, and where black patients were treated with dignity.

Due to Daniel's efforts, Provident Hospital was opened in 1891. It had both black and white doctors on staff, and it also had a nurses' training school. It was the first inter-racial hospital in the United States.

Two years later, Daniel performed an operation that made him famous world-wide. A man who had been stabbed in the chest was rushed to Provident Hospital. Daniel had to cut into the man's chest to remove the knife and sew up the wound. This operation had been done before, but the patient had always died. Daniel's patient survived. Daniel had performed the world's first successful heart operation. His success was partly because his instruments were so carefully sterilized.

During his next appointment as surgeon-in-chief of the Freedmen's Hospital in Washington, D.C., he was equally careful about keeping everything germ-free. During his first year at the Freedmen's, Daniel operated on 533 patients, only eight of whom died. This was an amazing record for those days.

"Before Dr. Williams came to the Freedmen's Hospital in 1894, there was no real surgical department. It can be said that with the arrival of Dr. Williams, surgical development began in all forms."
– William A. Warfield

Accomplishments

1883 Received M.D. from Chicago Medical College.

1889 Appointed to Illinois State Board of Health.

1891 Opened Provident Hospital, Chicago.

1893 Performed the world's first successful heart operation.

1894-98 Surgeon-in-Chief of Freedmen's Hospital, Washington, D.C.

1895 Helped form the inter-racial Medico-Chirurgical Society of Washington. Also helped organize the National Medical Association and served as its first vice-president.

1913 Founding member of the American College of Surgeons.

Overcoming Obstacles

Daniel's success did not please everybody. Like all people who are ahead of their time, he suffered a lot of criticism. This was especially true during his years at the Freedmen's Hospital.

Provident Hospital provided work and training for nurses of all ethnic backgrounds. These nurses were celebrating the tenth anniversary of their 1894 graduation from Provident.

The Freedmen's Hospital had been set up for African Americans after the Civil War. Since it had no white patients, it received little money from the federal government. It was in terrible condition when Daniel took over as chief surgeon. There were no trained nurses on staff. The wards were five wooden sheds. Everything was run down and grubby.

Daniel set to work to clean up the hospital. He organized it into seven departments. He built up a staff of both black and white doctors. He lectured, held open surgery clinics, and performed many successful operations. As a result of his efforts, the hospital gained a great reputation and began to attract more patients.

Many people appreciated these reforms, but some of the staff objected to the changes. They felt things had been fine as they were. There were problems, too, with some of the white doctors. They did not like working for an African American.

When Daniel became a surgeon at an all-white hospital in 1913, he again experienced people's jealousy. Some of the white staff members were unable to accept an African-American chief surgeon. However, he was respected by his patients and admired by most colleagues.

When the National Medical Association was formed in 1895, Daniel was offered the position of president. He declined, but he agreed to serve as vice-president. It was fitting that Daniel should be an officer of this national organization. Among his many activities, he had visited twenty states, helping to set up more than forty hospitals for African-American patients.

Daniel was a founding member of the American College of Surgeons.

Daniel was also honored when the American College of Surgeons was formed in 1913. The college was limited to a hundred members, and Daniel was invited to be one of them. He was the only African American in the group.

Special Interests

- Daniel was very fond of music. He used to play the bass viol at charity events.

Frederick Douglass

Frederick realized how important reading was. He could read quite well by the age of fifteen.

Born a slave in Maryland, Frederick was taken from his mother when he was just a few months old. He saw her only four or five times after that. He grew up on a neighboring plantation where he and the other slave children were treated like animals. They slept on the floor, and their food was poured into a trough.

In 1825, when Frederick was eight, he was sent to Baltimore to be a servant to his master's relatives. There, for the first time, he was happy. He was fed and clothed well, and the mistress of the house taught him to read. Her husband objected, saying that a slave "should know nothing but to obey his master—to do as he is told." This made Frederick realize how important reading was. He could read quite well by the time he left Baltimore at the age of fifteen.

Back on his owner's plantation, Frederick began to teach other slaves. He tried to start a Sunday school. It was quickly closed by the master. Frederick was labeled a "troublemaker" and was sent to work for a farmer who was known for his cruelty.

Determined not to give in, Frederick kept up his reading and taught the other slaves to read. But he suffered such terrible floggings that he tried to escape. Punished again and jailed, he was later sent to work in a shipyard. In 1838, at the age of twenty-one, Frederick at last escaped. Disguising himself as a free, black sailor, he made his way to the northern states where slavery had been abolished.

Frederick settled in New Bedford, Massachusetts, and worked as a laborer. He married a free, black woman and was happier than he had ever been. But he often thought of the many who were still slaves in the South and was determined to help free them. In 1841, he spoke at an anti-slavery meeting on Nantucket Island. His listeners were white and were horrified to hear about all he had suffered.

Frederick so impressed his audience that the Massachusetts Anti-Slavery Society hired him as a lecturer. After he published his popular book *Narrative of the Life of Frederick Douglass* (1845), the Anti-Slavery Society feared that someone might capture him and return him to his owner for a reward. They helped him escape to Britain where he continued to lecture. Within two years, he had earned enough money to buy his freedom from his former owner.

Personality Profile

Career: Leader of the anti-slavery movement.

Born: February 1817, in Talbot County, Maryland, to Harriet Bailey and a white slave owner.

Died: February 20, 1895, in Washington, D.C.

By the time the Civil War broke out in 1861, Frederick was one of the best-known African Americans in the country. He supported the war in his writings and lectures and helped recruit African-American soldiers for the Union army. After the war, he was appointed to the legislature of the District of Columbia. In 1877, he was made marshal of the District of Columbia. He later served as U.S. consul general to the Republic of Haiti.

Throughout his life, Frederick continued to speak up for African Americans. Although slavery had been abolished, blacks were still not treated the same as whites. Frederick not only spoke against racism, but he proved by his own actions that he would not accept inequality. Two years after his first wife died, he married a white woman. This shocked many white people. Frederick calmly told them, "My first wife was the color of my mother, and the second, the color of my father."

Accomplishments

1838 Escaped from slavery.

1841 Hired as a lecturer by Massachusetts Anti-Slavery Society.

1845 Published *Narrative of the Life of Frederick Douglass*.

1845-47 Traveled and lectured on slavery in the British Isles.

1847 Started his first newspaper, the *North Star*.

1877 Appointed marshal of the District of Columbia.

1889-91 Served as U.S. consul general to Haiti.

Fannie Lou Hamer

HUMAN RIGHTS
"No American can rest while any American is denied his rights...."

Growing up on a plantation in Sunflower County, Mississippi, Fannie often wondered why life was so unfair. Why was it that whites had all the fun, and black people did all the work? Her parents were sharecroppers—farmers who worked for a plantation owner. They had so little money that they had difficulty feeding and clothing their children.

The youngest of twenty children, Fannie began to work in the cotton fields when she was six. The plantation owner got her to pick more and more cotton by promising her candies and fruit, treats Fannie's family could not begin to afford. She worked harder and harder and was picking 400 pounds of cotton a week by the time she was thirteen.

Fannie often wondered why life was so unfair.

Like most sharecroppers' children, Fannie had little education. She went to school only between December and March when black workers were not needed in the cotton fields. If the weather was cold, Fannie had to stay at home because her family could not afford to buy her warm clothes. When Fannie grew up, she continued to work on the plantation, living in poverty and hardship. However, her life began to change in 1962, when she was forty-five years old.

In the early 1960s, civil rights groups tried to get more African Americans to vote. Without the vote, African Americans had no say in how the country was governed, and so most laws favored whites. Almost half the people in Mississippi were black, yet nearly all the voters were white. Many white people did not want this to change. So when African Americans tried to register for the vote, they were often given a very hard time.

Fannie and some friends tried to register for the vote in 1962. On the way home, they were fined for traveling in a school bus that was "too yellow." The authorities were just looking for an excuse to harass Fannie and her friends.

Personality Profile

Career: Sharecropper and civil rights activist.

Born: October 6, 1917, in Montgomery County, Mississippi, to Jim and Ella Townsend.

Died: March 15, 1977, in Mound Bayou, Mississippi.

Awards: Fifth Avenue Baptist Church, 1963; honorary degree from Tougaloo College, 1969; National Sojourner Truth Meritorious Service Award; Voter Registration Award, Nashville, Tennessee; many honorary degrees.

When the plantation owner heard about this, he fired Fannie and her family. Her life was threatened, and the house she fled to was riddled with bullets. All these problems happened just because she had tried to register to vote.

After this, Fannie devoted her life to the civil rights struggle. She helped African Americans register to vote, and she worked hard to improve the lives of needy black families. This took a great deal of courage. On one occasion, Fannie was thrown into jail and badly beaten for trying to enter a whites-only restaurant.

Fannie tried to run for Congress but was not successful. She remained a public figure and, until the end of her life, gave speeches to make life better for African Americans. She was famous for saying, "I'm sick and tired of being sick and tired." The hard-working sharecroppers of the South knew exactly what she meant. They, too, were tired of the way things were. They wanted a better life for themselves and their children.

Accomplishments

1962 First attempt to vote.

1963 Started Delta Ministry, a community development program.

1964 Helped found the Mississippi Freedom Democratic Party and attended the Democratic Convention.

1964 Unsuccessful attempt to run for Congress.

1968 Official delegate to the Democratic Convention.

1969 Founded Freedom Farms Corporation to help needy families.

Garrett Morgan

G arrett left his home in the mountains of Kentucky when he was fourteen. He had only a grade five education. The nearest big city was Cincinnati, Ohio, and he hoped to find work there. He got a job as a handyman.

When Garrett was eighteen, he moved north to a bigger city—Cleveland, Ohio. There he taught himself how sewing machines worked so that he could get a job repairing them. For the next few years, Garrett worked as a sewing-machine mechanic. As he oiled and serviced the machines, he realized they could use some improvements. By 1901, he had invented a belt fastener for the machines.

Garrett saved enough money to open his own sewing-machine repair shop in 1907. It did so well that he was able to start a tailoring business, making dresses and suits. This led to his most successful invention. It happened by accident.

Garrett's workers were having problems sewing woolen material. When the sewing machines ran fast, the needles became hot and burnt the wool. Garrett invented a cream to put on the wool so that the needles would easily slip through the cloth and not get hot. One night, when leaving in a hurry, he wiped some of the cream off his hands on a cloth of curly pony hair. When he returned the next day, he saw that the pony hair had gone straight. Garrett had discovered a hair straightener.

To make sure that the cream really worked, Garrett tried it on a friend's dog. Its fur went straight, and the dog suffered no harm. Next, Garrett tried it on his own head. His hair went straight. Here was a product that many people would love to have. It made Garrett a fortune.

Personality Profile

Career: Inventor.

Born: March 4, 1877, in Paris, Kentucky, to Sidney and Elizabeth Morgan.

Died: July 27, 1963, in Cleveland, Ohio.

Awards and honors: First Grand Prize Golden Medal at the International Exposition of Safety and Sanitation, 1914; honorary member of the International Association of Fire Engineers; U.S. government citation for his traffic signal; a public school in Harlem was named for him, 1976.

Next, Garrett invented a gas mask to help firefighters in smoke-filled buildings. For two years, he worked on improving this "breathing device." Its biggest test was on July 24, 1916. An explosion in a tunnel under Lake Erie had trapped about two dozen men. Garrett and his brother put on their gas masks and went down into the smoke-filled tunnel. One by one, they pulled out the trapped men and saved more than twenty lives. Garrett was awarded a gold medal for his bravery. In World War I, these gas masks protected soldiers from poison gas.

Garrett also invented the three-way, automatic traffic light. Before this, there used to be only "stop" and "go" lights on traffic signals. There was no yellow light to warn drivers that the signal was going to change. As a result, there were many bad accidents at crossroads. Garrett's invention saved many lives.

Garrett also did much for his community. He started a black newspaper, *Cleveland Call*, because he believed the Cleveland papers did not report enough news about African Americans.

In 1943, when Garrett was in his sixties, he began to go blind. For the last twenty years of his life, he could hardly see. Still, he kept busy. A highly respected member of the community, he was supported by his many friends and admirers.

Accomplishments

1901 Sold his first invention, a belt fastener for sewing machines.

1907 Started his own sewing-machine business.

1909 Began a tailoring business.

1912 Invented the gas mask.

1913 Formed the Morgan Hair Refining Cream company to sell his hair straightener.

1914 Formed the National Safety Device Company to make gas masks.

1914 First Grand Prize by the National Safety Device Company.

1920 Established a black newspaper, *Cleveland Call*.

1922 Invented the three-way traffic signal.

1931 Ran for office in Cleveland city council.

Sojourner Truth

Sojourner means traveler. Sojourner chose this name for herself late in life when she became a traveling preacher. As a child, she was a slave called Bell. She never knew most of her brothers and sisters. They were sold before she was born. In about 1806, when she was nine, Sojourner herself was sold for a hundred dollars at an auction.

Sojourner was mistreated by her new master. She was sold twice more until she ended up with a family called Dumont in New Paltz, New York. At the age of fourteen, she married one of the Dumont's slaves, an older man called Thomas.

Some years later, New York State passed a law that all slaves in the state must be freed before 1828. Dumont said he would free Sojourner a year early, but he did not keep his promise. Feeling betrayed, Sojourner fled to New York City, taking her baby daughter with her. She found work as a servant with Isaac and Maria Van Wagenen who paid Dumont twenty dollars for Sojourner's freedom.

"Dat man ober dar say dat womin needs to be helped into carriages, and lifted ober ditches, and to hab the best place everywhar. Nobody eber helps me into carriages, or ober mudpuddles, or gibs me any best place! And a'n't I a woman?"

Although Sojourner was now free, her son Peter was not. He had been sold to a slave owner in Alabama. It was against New York law for slaves to be sold to another state, so Sojourner sued the slave owner. With the help of a group of Quakers, Peter was returned. It was one of the first cases of a black woman winning a case against a white man.

Around this time, Sojourner became very religious. She began to preach at church meetings, and in 1832, she became a follower of a man called Matthias who claimed to be God. Sojourner was the only African American in Matthias's group. She gave him her life's savings so that they could all live together in a commune. For a while, all went well, but two years later, the commune broke up, and Sojourner lost everything.

For the next few years, Sojourner supported herself by doing housework. Meanwhile, she became an active member of the African Zion Church in New York City. Then one day in 1843, she thought she heard a voice from God instructing her to leave the city and "travel up and down the land," telling people about their sins. This was when she took the name Sojourner Truth.

During her journeys as a traveling preacher, Sojourner met some of America's leading abolitionists—people who were trying to put an end to slavery. She also met the leading feminists—people who were trying to get equal rights for women. Sojourner eagerly took up both causes, preaching their message on her travels.

Personality Profile

Career: Anti-slavery leader and preacher.

Born: Isabella Baumfree, about 1797, in Ulster County, New York, to James and Elizabeth Baumfree.

Died: November 26, 1883, in Battle Creek, Michigan.

By this time, Sojourner was famous throughout the country. She was an impressive woman—more than six feet tall with a deep, rich singing voice. Although she spoke in simple language, her words were always to the point. She was a key speaker at large conventions, and in 1864, she went to Washington where she met President Lincoln.

After the Civil War, Sojourner tried to get Congress to set aside a large piece of land in the West for freed slaves. She thought there should be one African-American state. Although she failed in this goal, she did much to help the freed slaves. Even when she was in her eighties, she was still an active reformer.

Sojourner's health failed her in 1879. She died in 1883 in Battle Creek, Michigan, where she is buried. She was one of the most important African-American women of her time.

Accomplishments

1832 Joined Matthias's religious sect.

1843 Took the name Sojourner Truth and became a traveling preacher.

1849 Went on a lecture tour against slavery.

1850 Published her life story, *Narrative of Sojourner Truth*.

1851 Spoke at a women's rights conference in Akron, Ohio.

1863 Went to Washington to help black refugees from the South during the Civil War.

1870 Presented a petition to Congress asking for a grant of land for former slaves.

Booker T. Washington

Booker longed to learn to read. His wish was granted in 1865 when the Civil War ended.

B ooker's first home was a crowded one-room cabin with a dirt floor. Like his mother and his brother and sister, he was a slave of the Burroughs family. He was put to work as soon as he was able to hold a broom and carry a bucket.

One of Booker's many tasks was to carry the schoolbooks of the Burroughs's son. Day after day, as he walked with the boy to school, he wished that he, too, could attend classes. He longed to learn to read. Booker's wish was granted in 1865 when the Civil War ended. After his family was freed, his mother moved to Malden, West Virginia, and there Booker began his schooling. But this education did not last long. After a few months, his mother died, and Booker had to go to work. He was barely ten years old. Booker did heavy laboring jobs in the salt pits and then in a coal mine.

When he was fourteen, Booker got a job as a houseboy for the mine-owner's wife, Viola Rulfner. Not only was this easier work, but also Mrs. Rulfner allowed him time to study. She thought an education was very important, even for slaves.

Two years later, in 1872, Booker heard about the Hampton Institute, a school that had recently been opened for African Americans. Although it was 500 miles away, Booker was determined to study there. Gathering together his savings, he walked almost all the way. He had just fifty cents left when he arrived.

Booker spent three years at Hampton. To pay for his education, he worked as a janitor. He graduated with honors in 1875. Booker spent another year studying at a school in Washington, D.C., before returning to Hampton as a teacher. He was an enthusiastic teacher. He inspired his students with his own love of learning. Booker gained such a reputation that, in 1881, he was chosen to be the first principal of Tuskegee Institute in Alabama.

Personality Profile

Career: Teacher.

Born: April 5, 1856, near Hale's Ford, Virginia, to Jane Ferguson and a white slave owner.

Died: November 14, 1915, in Tuskegee, Alabama.

Awards: Honorary degree from Harvard University, 1896.

When Booker arrived at the school, he found thirty students but no buildings. He started giving lessons in a shed. It was difficult at first. Students often had to build their own classrooms. Soon, Booker convinced wealthy business people to give money to the college. He hired talented teachers, such as the agriculturalist George Washington Carver. Slowly, the school grew and prospered.

Tuskegee Institute specialized in practical training. Booker believed that African Americans would do best if they learned useful skills. He said that blacks should be content to have a good job and earn good wages. This attitude made him popular with whites but was strongly criticized by many African Americans. Booker actually believed that blacks and whites should be treated equally. But he realized he would get more support for his college if he did not call for reforms too quickly.

His strategy worked. Powerful, white millionaires poured money into Tuskegee Institute. By the time Booker died, the college had a large campus of well-equipped buildings. It had 200 teachers and more than 2,000 regular students. As well, it was fast becoming a world-famous center for agricultural research.

Accomplishments

1875 Graduated with honors from the Hampton Institute.

1881 Appointed principal of the Tuskegee Institute.

1884 Gave speech to the National Education Association.

1895 Gave speech at the International Exposition in Atlanta.

1896 Showed President McKinley around Tuskegee Institute.

1901 Dined at the White House with President Theodore Roosevelt.

Ida B. Wells-Barnett

Born in 1862, during the Civil War, Ida grew up in Holly Springs, Mississippi, where her family had been slaves before the war. She attended Rust College in Holly Springs, a school for newly freed slaves. Ida enjoyed her school years—until tragedy struck. When she was sixteen, both her parents and one of her brothers died of yellow fever. Ida was left to bring up her five brothers and sisters. Since she urgently needed a job, she studied for the teachers' exam and was soon teaching at a school a few miles from home. The following year, she found a better teaching job in Memphis, Tennessee.

When she was just twenty-two, Ida sued the Southwestern Railroad Company. She had bought a ticket for the ladies' coach, but the conductor said she had to move to another part of the train. He did not want an African American in the ladies' coach. Ida was forced to leave the train. She sued the company, won her case, and was rewarded five hundred dollars. However, the railroad appealed, and the decision was reversed.

Personality Profile

Career: Journalist and social activist.

Born: July 16, 1862, in Holly Springs, Mississippi, to James and Elizabeth Wells.

Died: March 25, 1931, in Chicago, Illinois.

Honors: The Ida B. Wells-Barnett Housing Project was opened in Chicago, 1941; Chicago named her one of the twenty-five most outstanding women in the city's history, 1950; the U.S. Postal Service issued a stamp honoring her, 1990.

During the 1880s, Ida wrote for various black newspapers, always speaking out against injustice. In 1889, she became editor of the paper *Free Speech and Headlight*. She continued to teach school in Memphis—but not for long. When she wrote an article about the poor conditions in black schools, the white school board fired her.

Ida attracted national attention when she began to write about lynching. In 1892, three of Ida's friends were lynched—the men were taken from jail and hanged. They were respectable members of the black community and had done nothing wrong. But they had gained white enemies because their grocery business had been doing better than the whites' grocery store. Ida decided to look into other cases of lynching, and she found that many of the victims had been murdered simply because they were African American and successful.

Ida's articles angered many whites. As a result, the *Free Speech* office was destroyed, and Ida received so many death threats that she left Memphis.

After moving to Chicago, Illinois, in 1893, Ida formed a number of associations to help African Americans. As part of her effort to get black women the right to vote, she attended a suffrage parade in Washington in 1913. But when she went to take her place with the Illinois group of marchers, she was told to join the other black women at the back of the parade.

Ida had no intention of doing so. After all, she was representing Illinois, just like the white women. So she waited among the spectators, and when the parade was marching down Pennsylvania Avenue, she stepped out boldly and took her place among the whites. With actions such as this, Ida continued to fight racism until the end of her life.

Accomplishments

1884 Sued the Southwestern Railroad Company.

1884-91 Taught in Memphis schools.

1889 Became editor of the *Free Speech and Headlight*.

1892 Wrote first article against lynching and toured England.

1893 Organized Ida B. Wells Club which started a black orchestra and a black kindergarten in Chicago.

1894 Second tour of England.

1910 Formed the Negro Fellowship League to help out-of-work African Americans.

1913 Organized the Alpha Suffrage Club aimed at getting women the vote. Marched in suffrage parade in Washington, D.C.

Index

5 6 7 8 9 0 Printed in the United States 6 5 4 3